Hello!

THIS BOOK BELONGS TO:

TODAY I AM

HEIGHT:

WEIGHT:

WHEN I GROW UP I
WANT TO BE:

YEARS OLD

DATE:

MY SIGNATURE:

BEST FRIENDS:

FAVORITES

ANIMAL:

FOOD:

BOOK:

MY BEST QUALITY:

MOVIE:

GAME:

I LIKE LEARNING
ABOUT:

SONG:

SPORT/ACTIVITY:

I'M GOOD AT:

ONE THING
THAT MAKES
ME HAPPY:

IS MY HERO.

QUESTIONS & ANSWERS

> SOMETHING I WANT TO TRY THIS YEAR >

> SOMEWHERE I WANT TO TRAVEL >

> ACTIVITY I ENJOY DOING WITH FAMILY >

> SOMETHING I WANT TO MASTER THIS YEAR >

> SOMETHING I'M AFRAID OF >

> I NEVER LEAVE HOME WITHOUT >

> THREE WORDS THAT DESCRIBE ME >

>

>

> BEST PART OF THIS YEAR >

A QUICK NOTE FROM

TODAY I AM

HEIGHT:

WEIGHT:

WHEN I GROW UP I
WANT TO BE:

YEARS OLD

DATE:

MY SIGNATURE:

BEST FRIENDS:

FAVORITES

ANIMAL:

FOOD:

MY BEST QUALITY:

BOOK:

MOVIE:

GAME:

I LIKE LEARNING
ABOUT:

SONG:

SPORT/ACTIVITY:

I'M GOOD AT:

ONE THING
THAT MAKES
ME HAPPY:

IS MY HERO.

QUESTIONS & ANSWERS

> SOMETHING I WANT TO TRY THIS
> YEAR

> SOMEWHERE I WANT TO TRAVEL

> ACTIVITY I ENJOY DOING WITH
> FAMILY

> SOMETHING I WANT TO MASTER
> THIS YEAR

> SOMETHING I'M AFRAID OF

> I NEVER LEAVE HOME WITHOUT

> THREE WORDS THAT DESCRIBE
> ME

> BEST PART OF THIS YEAR

SNAPSHOTS

A QUICK NOTE FROM

TODAY I AM

HEIGHT:
WEIGHT:

WHEN I GROW UP I
WANT TO BE:

YEARS OLD

MY SIGNATURE:

DATE:

BEST FRIENDS:

MY BEST QUALITY:

I LIKE LEARNING
ABOUT:

I'M GOOD AT:

FAVORITES

ANIMAL:

FOOD:

BOOK:

MOVIE:

GAME:

SONG:

SPORT/ACTIVITY:

ONE THING
THAT MAKES
ME HAPPY:

IS MY HERO.

QUESTIONS & ANSWERS

⟩ SOMETHING I WANT TO TRY THIS YEAR ⟩

⟩ SOMEWHERE I WANT TO TRAVEL ⟩

⟩ ACTIVITY I ENJOY DOING WITH FAMILY ⟩

⟩ SOMETHING I WANT TO MASTER THIS YEAR ⟩

⟩ SOMETHING I'M AFRAID OF ⟩

⟩ I NEVER LEAVE HOME WITHOUT ⟩

⟩ THREE WORDS THAT DESCRIBE ME ⟩
⟩
⟩

⟩ BEST PART OF THIS YEAR ⟩

SNAPSHOTS

A QUICK NOTE FROM

TODAY I AM

HEIGHT:

WEIGHT:

WHEN I GROW UP I
WANT TO BE:

YEARS OLD

MY SIGNATURE:

DATE:

BEST FRIENDS:

FAVORITES

ANIMAL:

FOOD:

MY BEST QUALITY:

BOOK:

MOVIE:

GAME:

I LIKE LEARNING
ABOUT:

SONG:

SPORT/ACTIVITY:

I'M GOOD AT:

ONE THING
THAT MAKES
ME HAPPY:

IS MY HERO.

QUESTIONS & ANSWERS

> SOMETHING I WANT TO TRY THIS YEAR >

> SOMEWHERE I WANT TO TRAVEL >

> ACTIVITY I ENJOY DOING WITH FAMILY >

> SOMETHING I WANT TO MASTER THIS YEAR >

> SOMETHING I'M AFRAID OF >

> I NEVER LEAVE HOME WITHOUT >

> THREE WORDS THAT DESCRIBE ME >

> >

> >

> BEST PART OF THIS YEAR >

SNAPSHOTS

A QUICK NOTE FROM

TODAY I AM

HEIGHT:

WEIGHT:

WHEN I GROW UP I
WANT TO BE:

YEARS OLD

MY SIGNATURE:

DATE:

BEST FRIENDS:

MY BEST QUALITY:

I LIKE LEARNING
ABOUT:

I'M GOOD AT:

FAVORITES

ANIMAL:

FOOD:

BOOK:

MOVIE:

GAME:

SONG:

SPORT/ACTIVITY:

ONE THING
THAT MAKES
ME HAPPY:

IS MY HERO.

QUESTIONS & ANSWERS

➤ SOMETHING I WANT TO TRY THIS YEAR ➤

➤ SOMEWHERE I WANT TO TRAVEL ➤

➤ ACTIVITY I ENJOY DOING WITH FAMILY ➤

➤ SOMETHING I WANT TO MASTER THIS YEAR ➤

➤ SOMETHING I'M AFRAID OF ➤

➤ I NEVER LEAVE HOME WITHOUT ➤

➤ THREE WORDS THAT DESCRIBE ME ➤

➤

➤

➤ BEST PART OF THIS YEAR ➤

SNAPSHOTS

A QUICK NOTE FROM

TODAY I AM

HEIGHT:

WEIGHT:

WHEN I GROW UP I
WANT TO BE:

YEARS OLD

MY SIGNATURE:

DATE:

BEST FRIENDS:

FAVORITES

ANIMAL:

FOOD:

BOOK:

MY BEST QUALITY:

MOVIE:

GAME:

SONG:

I LIKE LEARNING
ABOUT:

SPORT/ACTIVITY:

I'M GOOD AT:

ONE THING
THAT MAKES
ME HAPPY:

IS MY HERO.

QUESTIONS & ANSWERS

SOMETHING I WANT TO TRY THIS YEAR

SOMEWHERE I WANT TO TRAVEL

ACTIVITY I ENJOY DOING WITH FAMILY

SOMETHING I WANT TO MASTER THIS YEAR

SOMETHING I'M AFRAID OF

I NEVER LEAVE HOME WITHOUT

THREE WORDS THAT DESCRIBE ME

BEST PART OF THIS YEAR

A QUICK NOTE FROM

TODAY I AM

HEIGHT:

WEIGHT:

WHEN I GROW UP I
WANT TO BE:

YEARS OLD

MY SIGNATURE:

DATE:

BEST FRIENDS:

FAVORITES

ANIMAL:

FOOD:

BOOK:

MY BEST QUALITY:

MOVIE:

GAME:

I LIKE LEARNING
ABOUT:

SONG:

SPORT/ACTIVITY:

I'M GOOD AT:

ONE THING
THAT MAKES
ME HAPPY:

IS MY HERO.

QUESTIONS & ANSWERS

> SOMETHING I WANT TO TRY THIS YEAR

> SOMEWHERE I WANT TO TRAVEL

> ACTIVITY I ENJOY DOING WITH FAMILY

> SOMETHING I WANT TO MASTER THIS YEAR

> SOMETHING I'M AFRAID OF

> I NEVER LEAVE HOME WITHOUT

> THREE WORDS THAT DESCRIBE ME

> BEST PART OF THIS YEAR

SNAPSHOTS

A QUICK NOTE FROM

TODAY I AM

HEIGHT:

WEIGHT:

WHEN I GROW UP I
WANT TO BE:

YEARS OLD

MY SIGNATURE:

DATE:

BEST FRIENDS:

FAVORITES

ANIMAL:

FOOD:

BOOK:

MY BEST QUALITY:

MOVIE:

GAME:

I LIKE LEARNING
ABOUT:

SONG:

SPORT/ACTIVITY:

I'M GOOD AT:

ONE THING
THAT MAKES
ME HAPPY:

IS MY HERO.

QUESTIONS & ANSWERS

⟩ SOMETHING I WANT TO TRY THIS YEAR ⟩

⟩ SOMEWHERE I WANT TO TRAVEL ⟩

⟩ ACTIVITY I ENJOY DOING WITH FAMILY ⟩

⟩ SOMETHING I WANT TO MASTER THIS YEAR ⟩

⟩ SOMETHING I'M AFRAID OF ⟩

⟩ I NEVER LEAVE HOME WITHOUT ⟩

⟩ THREE WORDS THAT DESCRIBE ME ⟩

⟩

⟩

⟩ BEST PART OF THIS YEAR ⟩

SNAPSHOTS

A QUICK NOTE FROM

TODAY I AM

HEIGHT:

WEIGHT:

WHEN I GROW UP I
WANT TO BE:

YEARS OLD

MY SIGNATURE:

DATE:

BEST FRIENDS:

FAVORITES

ANIMAL:

FOOD:

BOOK:

MY BEST QUALITY:

MOVIE:

GAME:

SONG:

I LIKE LEARNING
ABOUT:

SPORT/ACTIVITY:

I'M GOOD AT:

ONE THING
THAT MAKES
ME HAPPY:

IS MY HERO.

QUESTIONS & ANSWERS

> SOMETHING I WANT TO TRY THIS YEAR >

> SOMEWHERE I WANT TO TRAVEL >

> ACTIVITY I ENJOY DOING WITH FAMILY >

> SOMETHING I WANT TO MASTER THIS YEAR >

> SOMETHING I'M AFRAID OF >

> I NEVER LEAVE HOME WITHOUT >

> THREE WORDS THAT DESCRIBE ME >

>

>

> BEST PART OF THIS YEAR >

A QUICK NOTE FROM

TODAY I AM

HEIGHT:

WEIGHT:

WHEN I GROW UP I
WANT TO BE:

YEARS OLD

MY SIGNATURE:

DATE:

BEST FRIENDS:

MY BEST QUALITY:

**I LIKE LEARNING
ABOUT:**

FAVORITES

ANIMAL:

FOOD:

BOOK:

MOVIE:

GAME:

SONG:

SPORT/ACTIVITY:

I'M GOOD AT:

**ONE THING
THAT MAKES
ME HAPPY:**

IS MY HERO.

QUESTIONS & ANSWERS

> SOMETHING I WANT TO TRY THIS YEAR >

> SOMEWHERE I WANT TO TRAVEL >

> ACTIVITY I ENJOY DOING WITH FAMILY >

> SOMETHING I WANT TO MASTER THIS YEAR >

> SOMETHING I'M AFRAID OF >

> I NEVER LEAVE HOME WITHOUT >

> THREE WORDS THAT DESCRIBE ME >

> >

> >

> BEST PART OF THIS YEAR >

SNAPSHOTS

A QUICK NOTE FROM

TODAY I AM

HEIGHT:
WEIGHT:

WHEN I GROW UP I
WANT TO BE:

YEARS OLD

DATE:

MY SIGNATURE:

BEST FRIENDS:

FAVORITES

ANIMAL:

FOOD:

MY BEST QUALITY:

BOOK:

MOVIE:

GAME:

I LIKE LEARNING
ABOUT:

SONG:

SPORT/ACTIVITY:

I'M GOOD AT:

ONE THING
THAT MAKES
ME HAPPY:

IS MY HERO.

QUESTIONS & ANSWERS

SOMETHING I WANT TO TRY THIS YEAR

SOMEWHERE I WANT TO TRAVEL

ACTIVITY I ENJOY DOING WITH FAMILY

SOMETHING I WANT TO MASTER THIS YEAR

SOMETHING I'M AFRAID OF

I NEVER LEAVE HOME WITHOUT

THREE WORDS THAT DESCRIBE ME

BEST PART OF THIS YEAR

SNAPSHOTS

A QUICK NOTE FROM

TODAY I AM

HEIGHT:

WEIGHT:

WHEN I GROW UP I
WANT TO BE:

YEARS OLD

MY SIGNATURE:

DATE:

BEST FRIENDS:

FAVORITES

ANIMAL:

FOOD:

BOOK:

MY BEST QUALITY:

MOVIE:

GAME:

SONG:

I LIKE LEARNING
ABOUT:

SPORT/ACTIVITY:

I'M GOOD AT:

ONE THING
THAT MAKES
ME HAPPY:

IS MY HERO.

QUESTIONS & ANSWERS

> SOMETHING I WANT TO TRY THIS YEAR >

> SOMEWHERE I WANT TO TRAVEL >

> ACTIVITY I ENJOY DOING WITH FAMILY >

> SOMETHING I WANT TO MASTER THIS YEAR >

> SOMETHING I'M AFRAID OF >

> I NEVER LEAVE HOME WITHOUT >

> THREE WORDS THAT DESCRIBE ME >

>

>

> BEST PART OF THIS YEAR >

SNAPSHOTS

A QUICK NOTE FROM

TODAY I AM

HEIGHT:

WEIGHT:

WHEN I GROW UP I
WANT TO BE:

YEARS OLD

MY SIGNATURE:

DATE:

BEST FRIENDS:

FAVORITES

ANIMAL:

FOOD:

BOOK:

MY BEST QUALITY:

MOVIE:

GAME:

SONG:

I LIKE LEARNING
ABOUT:

SPORT/ACTIVITY:

I'M GOOD AT:

ONE THING
THAT MAKES
ME HAPPY:

IS MY HERO.

QUESTIONS & ANSWERS

≫ SOMETHING I WANT TO TRY THIS YEAR ≫

≫ SOMEWHERE I WANT TO TRAVEL ≫

≫ ACTIVITY I ENJOY DOING WITH FAMILY ≫

≫ SOMETHING I WANT TO MASTER THIS YEAR ≫

≫ SOMETHING I'M AFRAID OF ≫

≫ I NEVER LEAVE HOME WITHOUT ≫

≫ THREE WORDS THAT DESCRIBE ME ≫

≫

≫

≫ BEST PART OF THIS YEAR ≫

A QUICK NOTE FROM

TODLAY I AM

HEIGHT:

WEIGHT:

WHEN I GROW UP I
WANT TO BE:

YEARS OLD

MY SIGNATURE:

DATE:

BEST FRIENDS:

FAVORITES

ANIMAL:

FOOD:

MY BEST QUALITY:

BOOK:

MOVIE:

GAME:

I LIKE LEARNING ABOUT:

SONG:

SPORT/ACTIVITY:

I'M GOOD AT:

ONE THING
THAT MAKES
ME HAPPY:

IS MY HERO.

QUESTIONS & ANSWERS

⟫ SOMETHING I WANT TO TRY THIS YEAR ⟫

⟫ SOMEWHERE I WANT TO TRAVEL ⟫

⟫ ACTIVITY I ENJOY DOING WITH FAMILY ⟫

⟫ SOMETHING I WANT TO MASTER THIS YEAR ⟫

⟫ SOMETHING I'M AFRAID OF ⟫

⟫ I NEVER LEAVE HOME WITHOUT ⟫

⟫ THREE WORDS THAT DESCRIBE ME ⟫

⟫

⟫

⟫ BEST PART OF THIS YEAR ⟫

SNAPSHOTS

A QUICK NOTE FROM

TODAY I AM

HEIGHT:
WEIGHT:

WHEN I GROW UP I
WANT TO BE:

YEARS OLD

MY SIGNATURE:

DATE:

BEST FRIENDS:

FAVORITES

ANIMAL:

FOOD:

BOOK:

MY BEST QUALITY:

MOVIE:

GAME:

I LIKE LEARNING
ABOUT:

SONG:

SPORT/ACTIVITY:

I'M GOOD AT:

ONE THING
THAT MAKES
ME HAPPY:

IS MY HERO.

QUESTIONS & ANSWERS

> SOMETHING I WANT TO TRY THIS YEAR >

> SOMEWHERE I WANT TO TRAVEL >

> ACTIVITY I ENJOY DOING WITH FAMILY >

> SOMETHING I WANT TO MASTER THIS YEAR >

> SOMETHING I'M AFRAID OF >

> I NEVER LEAVE HOME WITHOUT >

> THREE WORDS THAT DESCRIBE ME >
>
>

> BEST PART OF THIS YEAR >

A QUICK NOTE FROM

Made in the USA
Coppell, TX
30 July 2023

19763963R00038